BEAST MODE: THE UNTOLD STORY OF MRBEAST'S RISE TO FAME AND PHILANTHROPY

CONTENTS

INTRODUCTION

MrBeast, whose real name is Jimmy Donaldson, is a name synonymous with success, innovation, and philanthropy in the world of YouTube and social media. At just 23 years old, he has already built a massive following of over 100 million subscribers across his various channels, making him one of the most popular creators on the platform.

But MrBeast's journey to success was not without its challenges. Starting out as a teenager in a small town in North Carolina, he spent years creating videos and experimenting with different approaches, often with little success. It wasn't until he discovered his talent for creating over-the-top stunts and engaging with his audience in unique ways that his channel began to take off.

In the world of YouTube, MrBeast has redefined the limits of creativity and philanthropy, embodying a unique approach that sets him apart from his peers. His journey on the platform has showcased an unwavering commitment to hard work, determination, and a profound desire to make a positive impact on the world.

His reputation for pushing boundaries and exploring new frontiers is evident in his remarkable endeavors, from spearheading a monumental campaign to plant 20 million trees to organizing challenges that test the endurance of his fans, such as the captivating 'Finger on the App' game. His unyielding dedication to these ventures reflects his firm belief in the transformative power of unconventional ideas.

Beyond its role as a hub for entertainment and viral content, YouTube has emerged as a potent instrument for philanthropy. Influential creators who have adeptly leveraged the platform's extensive reach and influence to effect meaningful change in the world. With millions of subscribers and views, YouTube creators possess a distinctive ability to raise awareness and resources for diverse causes, thus amplifying their impact on a global scale.

MrBeast's pioneering philanthropic exploits have not only touched countless lives but have also ignited a wave of inspiration among a new cohort of creators, urging them to utilize their platforms for altruistic endeavors. Through his dedicated fan base and substantial following, He has epitomized the profound potential of YouTube as a force for positive transformation.

In 2012, MrBeast commenced his YouTube odyssey, initially delving into gaming and commentary videos, akin to many of his contemporaries. However, his distinctive persona and innovative concepts swiftly set him apart, propelling him to cultivate a devoted following and carve out a distinct identity on the platform. As he continued to innovate and experiment with diverse formats, MrBeast solidified his position as a trailblazer in the realm of YouTube content creation.

The challenge "Last YouTuber to Leave the Circle Wins $100,000" exemplified his creativity and deep commitment to effecting change. By intertwining entertainment with philanthropy, he not only engaged his audience but also supported charitable causes. This distinctive approach has positioned MrBeast as a singular creator in the YouTube sphere, profoundly impacting his audience. His acts of generosity have inspired countless individuals to believe in their capacity to make a difference, spurring many to initiate their own charitable endeavors or champion causes close to their hearts.

MrBeast's way of philanthropy hasn't just inspired action; it has fostered a sense of community among his viewers. By involving his audience in decision-making processes, he has cultivated a connection that transcends the digital realm. The extensive planning, coordination, and execution involved in his philanthropic pursuits offer a deeper understanding of the meticulousness and dedication underpinning each project.

Ensuring lasting impact is a key challenge for MrBeast's team. Through partnerships with local organizations and sustained commitments to specific causes, they strive to create sustainable change. As MrBeast's influence continues to burgeon, the release of his biography book is eagerly anticipated. Promising an intimate portrayal of his life and journey, the book will provide readers with unprecedented insights into his philanthropic endeavors, personal experiences, and the values propelling him.

The Beast Mode biography book delves into MrBeast's ascent to fame, offering a comprehensive account of his philanthropic initiatives and the motivations driving him. With never-before-revealed details and personal insights, the book promises an immersive experience for fans and aspiring creators alike. It also explores the strategies and principles that have underpinned MrBeast's success, offering valuable lessons for those seeking to make a difference in the world.

The release of Beast Mode book solidifies MrBeast's legacy, serving as an inspiration for readers to pursue their passions, challenge conventions, and utilize their platforms for positive change. It encapsulates not just one individual's story but also serves as a call to action for all to make a meaningful impact in the world, echoing MrBeast's extraordinary acts of generosity and unwavering dedication to philanthropy.

THE EARLY DAYS GROWING UP IN EASTERN NORTH CAROLINA

Jimmy Donaldson, better known by his online moniker "MrBeast," is one of the most successful and influential creators on YouTube today. But before he became a household name, he was just a kid growing up in Eastern North Carolina.

Jimmy's parents divorced when he was young, and he lived with his mother and brother in a small town outside of Greenville. As a child, he struggled with attention deficit hyperactivity disorder (ADHD) and found it difficult to focus in school. However, he excelled in computer classes and spent much of his free time playing video games and experimenting with different software programs.

As Jimmy grew older, his fascination with technology and innovation only intensified. He found himself drawn to the world of YouTube, where he could experiment with different types of content and editing techniques alongside his friends. Yet, despite his enthusiasm and drive, his channel initially struggled to gain traction, and Jimmy found himself struggling to find his creative voice.

However, rather than succumbing to self-doubt and despair, Jimmy doubled down on his passion and worked tirelessly to refine his craft as a content creator. He remained determined to develop his skills and find his place in the fiercely competitive landscape of YouTube, where success was measured not only by the quality of one's content, but also by the size of one's audience.

And indeed, Jimmy's tenacity and dedication paid off in ways he could never have imagined. His willingness to go to extreme lengths to entertain his audience and set the stage for the massive stunts and philanthropic efforts that he has become known for is a testament to his unwavering commitment to his craft and to his fans. In the end, it was Jimmy's unyielding passion and creative vision that propelled him to the forefront of the YouTube community and earned him the respect and admiration of millions of fans around the world.

This journey to success was not an easy one, and he relied heavily on the support of his close-knit group of friends and family throughout the process. In fact, it would not be an exaggeration to say that his supportive network played a crucial role in his development as a creator.

From a young age, Jimmy showed a keen interest in creating content and was always looking for new ways to express himself creatively. However, like many aspiring creators, he faced his fair share of challenges and setbacks along the way. It was during these difficult times that his friends and family stepped up to offer him the encouragement and support he needed to keep going.

For example, when Jimmy was just starting out on YouTube, he often felt discouraged by the slow growth of his channel and the negative comments from viewers. However, his friends and family were there to remind him of his potential and to encourage him to keep creating content that he was passionate about.

They also provided him with the resources he needed to succeed, such as lending him equipment to make better videos, helping him with video editing and brainstorming ideas for new content. Additionally, they often appeared in his videos, which helped to create a sense of community around his channel and made his content more relatable and engaging to his audience.

In the next chapter, we will explore how Jimmy discovered his passion for YouTube and how he developed his own unique style and voice on the platform.

FINDING HIS PASSION: HOW MRBEAST DISCOVERED YOUTUBE

As a teenager, Jimmy Donaldson, or "MrBeast" as he is known on YouTube, was interested in technology and computers. He spent hours playing video games and experimenting with different software programs. However, he never considered YouTube as a career option until he stumbled upon a few popular gaming channels on the platform.

The more MrBeast watched these videos, the more he became fascinated by the idea of creating his own content. He started by recording videos of himself playing video games and uploading them to his own YouTube channel. However, these early videos did not gain much traction, and he was discouraged by the lack of views and engagement.

Determined to succeed, MrBeast began to experiment

with different types of videos, including commentary on current events and popular internet memes. It wasn't until he uploaded a video titled "I Bought Every Billboard in My City For This" that he started to gain significant attention on the platform. The video went viral, and MrBeast's channel began to grow rapidly.

In the journey of MrBeast's rise to the summit of the YouTube platform, he encountered numerous challenges that tested his resolve as a content creator. Despite his initial success, he found himself grappling with the daunting task of producing innovative and captivating content that would engage his audience.

As he toiled to generate fresh ideas and push his creative boundaries, MrBeast was also subject to the harsh criticisms of viewers. The weight of negative comments and feedback threatened to shatter his confidence and deter his momentum.

But the greats are forged in the crucible of adversity. MrBeast, fortified by his unwavering determination, refused to surrender to the obstacles obstructing his path. Drawing from the support and resources of his closely-knit group of friends and family, he persisted in his pursuit of excellence, doggedly honing his craft and refining his vision.

While there were undoubtedly moments of discouragement and self-doubt, MrBeast persisted, unyielding in his quest to become a titan in the YouTube landscape. With a steadfast focus on his passion for entertaining and inspiring others, he steadily amassed a dedicated following that catapulted him to unprecedented heights of success.

In reflection, it was MrBeast's unwavering determination and commitment to his craft, combined with the invaluable support of his loved ones, that enabled him to overcome the challenges that threatened to derail his ascent. The indelible mark he has left on the platform stands as a testament to the enduring power of perseverance and resilience in the face of adversity.

As MrBeast's channel continued to gain traction, he quickly realized the importance of carving out a unique niche in the crowded landscape of YouTube. He knew that in order to stand out from the throngs of other creators vying for attention, he would need to develop a distinctive style and voice that resonated with his audience.

With characteristic audacity, MrBeast set about creating content that was both entertaining and attention-grabbing. His stunts and challenges often pushed the boundaries of what was considered acceptable on YouTube, with feats such as counting to 100,000 and spending 24 hours in a haunted house capturing the imaginations of his growing legion of fans.

But it wasn't just the sheer audacity of his stunts that drew viewers to MrBeast's channel. It was his unique approach to storytelling, which blended humor, suspense, and genuine emotional resonance to create a viewing experience that was truly one-of-a-kind. His infectious energy and irreverent humor brought a refreshing levity to the platform, earning him a dedicated following of fans who eagerly awaited his next outrageous escapade.

In many ways, MrBeast's rise to prominence is a testament to the power of creativity and originality in content creation. By daring to push the boundaries of what was considered acceptable on YouTube and developing a voice that was uniquely his own, he was able to capture the attention of millions of viewers and establish himself as one of the most successful content creators of our time.

In the next chapter, we will explore MrBeast's journey as he navigates the challenges of managing success and maintaining authenticity.

NAVIGATING SUCCESS: THE CHALLENGES OF MANAGING A GROWING AUDIENCE

As MrBeast's channel continued to experience exponential growth and he amassed a devoted following of fans, he soon found himself facing an entirely new set of challenges.

For one, he found himself increasingly pulled in different directions as he tried to balance the demands of his growing audience with his own desire to create content that was both impactful and meaningful. As he struggled to navigate these competing demands, MrBeast became acutely aware of the need to remain authentic as a creator, lest he risk losing the very audience that had propelled him to fame.

To overcome this challenge, MrBeast began to focus more on creating content that had a positive impact on the world, rather than simply relying on stunts and other gimmicks to generate views and clicks. He incorporated more charitable giving into his videos and launched campaigns to raise money for important causes such as environmental conservation and mental health awareness, cementing his reputation not only as a talented creator, but also as a conscientious and socially responsible individual.

Indeed, it was this commitment to making a positive difference in the world that helped MrBeast maintain his authenticity as a creator and continue to grow his audience, even as he faced new and increasingly complex challenges. In the end, it was MrBeast's unwavering dedication to his craft and his fans that allowed him to overcome these obstacles and cement his status as one of the most influential creators of his generation.

Another challenge that MrBeast faced was managing his personal brand and dealing with the scrutiny that came with his growing fame. He had to navigate criticism from viewers and the media, including accusations of clickbait and exploiting vulnerable individuals for content.

To address these challenges, MrBeast remained true to his values and focused on creating content that aligned with his mission of making the world a better place. He also surrounded himself with a close-knit group of friends and family who provided him with emotional support and helped him stay grounded.

Despite these challenges, MrBeast's channel continued to

grow, and he became one of the most successful creators on YouTube. His success was a testament to his hard work, dedication, and willingness to adapt and evolve as a creator.

In the next chapter, we will explore MrBeast's impact on the YouTube community and the broader world, as well as his plans for the future.

FROM LOCAL SENSATION TO WORLDWIDE PHENOMENON

In the age of social media, where content creators strive to capture the attention of millions, one name has risen above the rest - MrBeast. What started as a local sensation has now transformed into a worldwide phenomenon. The story of MrBeast's rise to fame is a testament to the power of determination and creativity.

What sets MrBeast apart from other content creators is his unwavering dedication to pushing the boundaries of what is possible. He consistently delivers content that is both entertaining and thought-provoking. Whether it's giving away thousands of dollars to strangers, organizing record-breaking challenges, or planting millions of trees, MrBeast's videos never fail to captivate his audience.

One of the key elements of MrBeast's content creation strategy is his ability to tap into the emotions of his viewers. He understands the power of storytelling and uses it to create a connection with his audience. By sharing personal stories and experiences, he invites his viewers to become a part of his journey, fostering a sense of loyalty and engagement.

A major factor in MrBeast's global reach is his strategic use of social media platforms. While YouTube is his primary platform, he has also expanded his presence on other platforms such as Instagram, Twitter, and TikTok. By diversifying his content and adapting it to each platform's unique format, MrBeast is able to reach a wider audience and engage with different demographics.

On Instagram, MrBeast shares behind-the-scenes glimpses into his life and the making of his videos. He leverages the platform's visual nature to showcase the impact of his philanthropic endeavors and create a sense of awe among his followers. Twitter, on the other hand, allows MrBeast to connect with his audience on a more personal level. He often shares updates, interacts with fans, and even organizes impromptu challenges through the platform.

YouTube has played a pivotal role in MrBeast's journey from a local sensation to a global phenomenon. With over 50 million subscribers and billions of views, his channel has become a hub for entertainment and inspiration. The platform's algorithm, combined with MrBeast's consistent uploading schedule and high-quality content, has helped him attract a massive audience.

MrBeast's videos are carefully crafted to keep viewers engaged from start to finish. He understands the importance of hooking the audience within the first few seconds and maintaining their interest throughout the video. From attention-grabbing thumbnails to compelling titles, MrBeast leaves no stone unturned in his quest to create content that resonates with his viewers and keeps them coming back for more.

Another key aspect of MrBeast's global reach is his collaborations with other popular influencers. By teaming up with creators who have a similar appeal and audience, he is able to tap into their fan base and introduce his content to new viewers. This cross-pollination of audiences has been instrumental in expanding MrBeast's reach and solidifying his position as a global sensation.

These collaborations often take the form of challenges or charity events, where multiple creators come together to achieve a common goal. By combining their efforts and leveraging their collective influence, MrBeast and his collaborators are able to make a significant impact on both social media and real-world issues. This collaborative approach not only benefits the creators involved but also creates a sense of community and camaraderie among their followers.

As MrBeast's influence continues to grow, it is clear that his global reach will only expand further. With his unwavering commitment to creating content that entertains, inspires, and makes a difference, he has become a role model for aspiring content creators worldwide. His philanthropic endeavors, in particular, have set a new standard for using social media as a force for good.

In the future, we can expect MrBeast to continue pushing boundaries and finding new ways to captivate his audience. Whether it's through groundbreaking challenges, innovative storytelling techniques, or even venturing into new platforms, MrBeast's global reach will undoubtedly continue to evolve and leave a lasting impact on the world of content creation.

From his humble beginnings as a local sensation to his current status as a worldwide phenomenon, MrBeast's journey is a testament to the power of creativity, determination, and authenticity. Through his unique content creation strategy, strategic use of social media platforms, collaborations with other influencers, and unwavering commitment to making a difference, he has captured the hearts and minds of millions.

As we look to the future, it is clear that MrBeast's global reach will only continue to expand. His impact extends far beyond the realm of entertainment, inspiring a new generation of content creators to use their platforms for good. MrBeast has proven that with a little creativity and a lot of passion, anyone can make a difference and leave a lasting impact on the world. So, let us join him on this journey and strive to make our own mark on the global stage.

DECODING MRBEAST:
A DEEP DIVE INTO
THE PERSONALITY

Traits that Set Him Apart

What sets MrBeast apart from other YouTubers? In this chapter , we will take a deep dive into the unique personality traits that have propelled him to success.

Authenticity:
One of the key aspects that sets MrBeast apart is his authenticity. Unlike many other influencers who rely on carefully curated personas, MrBeast presents himself as he is - a down-to-earth young man with a genuine desire to make a positive impact. This authenticity resonates with his audience, who appreciate his honesty and transparency. Whether he is giving away thousands of dollars to strangers or participating in outrageous challenges, it is clear that MrBeast's actions come from a

place of sincerity.

Determination:

Another notable personality trait of MrBeast is his unwavering determination. From his early days on YouTube, he has consistently pushed the boundaries of what is possible in the world of online content creation. Whether it's staying up for days on end to complete a challenge or investing countless hours into planning and executing his ambitious projects, MrBeast's determination is evident in every video he creates. This level of dedication has not only earned him a massive following but also inspired countless aspiring content creators.

Generosity:

Perhaps the most well-known personality trait of MrBeast is his remarkable generosity. He has made a name for himself by giving away extravagant sums of money to both individuals and charitable organizations. His acts of kindness have touched the lives of many, and his audience eagerly anticipates each new video to see how he will make a difference. MrBeast's generosity goes beyond monetary donations, as he often uses his platform to raise awareness for important causes and encourage others to give back. His philanthropic efforts have inspired a wave of positivity and kindness in the online community.

To truly understand the impact of MrBeast's personality traits, it is important to analyze the efforts he puts into his content. While his videos may appear to be spontaneous and lighthearted, there is a considerable amount of planning and strategizing that goes into each one.

MrBeast's videos often involve elaborate challenges and competitions, which require careful coordination and execution. Behind the scenes, a dedicated team of professionals works tirelessly to ensure that every detail is perfect. From scouting locations to securing permits, no stone is left unturned in the pursuit of creating captivating and memorable content.

In addition to his individual efforts, MrBeast also collaborates with other YouTubers and content creators to amplify his impact. By joining forces with like-minded individuals, he is able to reach a wider audience and create a greater positive change. This collaborative approach showcases MrBeast's ability to not only lead but also work well with others, further solidifying his position as a respected figure in the online community.

Beyond his YouTube channel, MrBeast has ventured into various business endeavors, showcasing his entrepreneurial spirit. He has launched merchandise lines, partnered with companies for brand sponsorships, and even started his own philanthropic organization. These ventures not only generate revenue but also allow him to expand his influence and make an even bigger impact.

MrBeast's success in the business world can be attributed to his ability to identify opportunities and take calculated risks. He understands the power of his brand and leverages it to forge partnerships that align with his values. This entrepreneurial mindset has not only contributed to his personal success but also allowed him to create opportunities for others. Through his collaborations and business ventures, he has helped to elevate the careers of fellow content creators and entrepreneurs.

MrBeast's unique personality traits and efforts have had a profound impact on his audience. His videos inspire viewers to dream big, to be kind, and to make a positive difference in the world. Many young people have been motivated to start their own YouTube channels, businesses, or charitable initiatives after being inspired by MrBeast's content.

Moreover, MrBeast's influence extends beyond the online realm. His philanthropic efforts have inspired others to give back and have sparked conversations about the importance of generosity and compassion. Through his videos, he has created a ripple effect of kindness that has touched countless lives.

While MrBeast is undoubtedly a trailblazer in the world of online content creation, there are other notable influencers who share similar personality traits. One such individual is Casey Neistat, a filmmaker and YouTuber known for his authentic storytelling and determination. Like MrBeast, Neistat's content is characterized by its honesty and the sheer effort he puts into every project.

Another influencer with similar traits is Emma Chamberlain, who rose to fame with her relatable and unfiltered vlogs. Chamberlain's authenticity and genuine personality have endeared her to her audience, much like MrBeast. Both influencers have managed to connect with their viewers on a personal level, creating a loyal and engaged following.

MrBeast's unique personality traits, including authenticity, determination, and generosity, have set him apart in the world of online content creation. His efforts, both on and off camera, have had a profound impact on his audience and have inspired a wave of positivity and kindness. As we continue to decode MrBeast, it is clear that his influence will continue to grow, leaving an indelible mark on the online community.

UNCOVERING THE BELIEFS AND MANTRAS THAT DRIVE MRBEAST'S SUCCESS

Success is a journey that is guided by the beliefs and mantras we embrace. These core principles shape our mindset, drive our actions, and ultimately determine our success. MrBeast, the popular YouTuber and philanthropist, has achieved remarkable success through his unwavering beliefs and powerful mantras. In this chapter, we will delve into the beliefs and mantras that have propelled MrBeast to the pinnacle of success, uncovering the secrets behind his rise to fame.

Beliefs and mantras serve as guiding principles that influence our decisions and actions. They are the foundational elements upon which success is built. MrBeast, known for his extravagant acts of generosity and his larger-than-life challenges, has a set of core beliefs that have been instrumental in his journey to success.

Belief #1: Giving Back is the Key to Success

One of MrBeast's core beliefs is that giving back to others is the key to achieving success. He firmly believes in the power of generosity and the impact it can have on people's lives. MrBeast's philanthropic efforts, such as donating thousands of dollars to random individuals or organizing charity events, exemplify his belief. By helping others and making a positive impact, MrBeast has not only gained a massive following but has also established himself as a role model for aspiring content creators.

Belief #2: Taking Risks and Thinking Big

MrBeast's success can be attributed to his belief in taking risks and thinking big. He doesn't shy away from pushing boundaries and venturing into uncharted territory. Whether it's attempting extreme challenges or creating unique content, MrBeast constantly pushes his limits. This belief in embracing risks and thinking outside the box has allowed him to stand out in a crowded digital landscape and capture the attention of millions.

Belief #3: The Importance of Hard Work and Persistence

Behind every successful individual lies a strong work ethic and unwavering persistence. MrBeast's belief in the value of hard work and persistence has been a driving force in his success. He dedicates countless hours to creating high-quality content and constantly strives to improve himself. This commitment to hard work, combined with his persistence in the face of challenges, has enabled MrBeast to achieve remarkable feats and reach new heights in his career.

Uncovering MrBeast's Mantras

In addition to his core beliefs, MrBeast also embraces powerful mantras that serve as daily reminders of his values and goals. These mantras shape his mindset and guide his actions, contributing to his continued success.

Mantra #1: "Push Your Limits and Never Settle"

MrBeast's first mantra is a call to constantly push one's limits and never settle for mediocrity. He believes that true growth and success can only be achieved by stepping outside of one's comfort zone and challenging oneself. By embracing this mantra, MrBeast has been able to consistently create content that captivates his audience and keeps them coming back for more.

Mantra #2: "Dream Big and Make It Happen"

Dreaming big is a mantra that MrBeast lives by. He encourages his followers to set audacious goals and work tirelessly to turn those dreams into reality. By believing in the power of dreams and taking massive action towards their fulfillment, MrBeast has transformed his own aspirations into a reality. This mantra serves as a reminder to his audience that anything is possible with the right mindset and determination.

Mantra #3: "Be Kind and Make a Positive Impact"

Kindness and making a positive impact on the world are at the core of MrBeast's third mantra. He strongly believes in the importance of being kind to others and using his influence to make a difference. This mantra is reflected in his charitable acts and philanthropic endeavors, which have touched the lives of countless individuals. By embodying kindness and striving to make a positive impact, MrBeast has garnered immense respect and admiration from his followers.

MrBeast's unwavering beliefs and powerful mantras have played a pivotal role in shaping his success. By embracing the belief that giving back is the key to success, he has not only built a loyal following but has also made a significant impact on the lives of others. His willingness to take risks and think big has set him apart from his peers, allowing him to capture the attention of millions. The importance he places on hard work and persistence has propelled him to achieve remarkable feats and reach new heights in his career.

MrBeast's success can be attributed to the beliefs and

mantras he holds dear. His core principles of giving back, taking risks, working hard, and being kind have guided his journey and shaped his remarkable achievements. By embracing these beliefs and mantras, we can learn valuable lessons that can drive our own success. So, let us be inspired by MrBeast and strive to uncover our own beliefs and mantras that will propel us to greatness.

THE POWER OF FRIENDSHIP: HOW MRBEAST'S INNER CIRCLE AND ROLE MODELS SHAPED HIS SUCCESS

Friendship is a powerful force that can shape our lives in profound ways. It provides us with emotional support, encouragement, and inspiration. In the case of Jimmy Donaldson, better known as MrBeast, his friendships have played a crucial role in his journey to success. MrBeast's inner circle, comprised of his closest friends, has been there for him every step of the way, providing unwavering support and helping him navigate the challenges of his career.

At the heart of MrBeast's success lies his inner circle, a group of friends who have been with him since the beginning. These individuals have not only been his closest confidants but have also played vital roles in his content creation. (Chris, Chandler, Garrett, and Jake are just a few of the core members of MrBeast's inner circle, each bringing their unique talents and perspectives to the table.)

Chris, in particular, has been MrBeast's right-hand man, helping him with brainstorming ideas, managing logistics, and even participating in some of the outrageous challenges that MrBeast is famous for. Chandler, known for his humorous antics, has become a beloved figure in MrBeast's videos, adding a touch of comedy to the content. Garrett and Jake, too, have made significant contributions, whether it's behind the scenes or in front of the camera.

Beyond his inner circle, MrBeast has also been influenced by several role models who have shaped his path to success. One such role model is Elon Musk, the visionary entrepreneur behind companies like Tesla and SpaceX. Musk's relentless pursuit of innovation and his audacious goals have inspired MrBeast to dream big and push the boundaries of what is possible.

Another influential figure in MrBeast's life is Warren Buffett, one of the most successful investors in history. Buffett's emphasis on long-term thinking and his commitment to giving back to society have left a lasting impact on MrBeast. He has adopted Buffett's philosophy of using wealth for the greater good, donating millions of dollars to charitable causes and organizing philanthropic initiatives.

MrBeast's inner circle and role models have imparted valuable lessons that have shaped his approach to content creation and his perspective on success. One of the key lessons he has learned is the importance of authenticity. MrBeast's videos are known for their genuine nature, and this authenticity stems from the close-knit relationship he shares with his friends. They have taught him that being true to oneself and staying grounded is crucial in an industry that often prioritizes image over substance.

Another lesson MrBeast has learned is the power of collaboration. His inner circle has shown him the value of working together as a team, pooling their strengths and talents to create content that resonates with their audience. This collaborative spirit has not only strengthened their friendship but has also elevated the quality of their videos.

MrBeast's friendships have had a profound influence on his content and career trajectory. His videos often revolve around challenges that involve his friends, showcasing the camaraderie and bond they share. This not only creates entertaining content but also reinforces the message of friendship and support that MrBeast holds dear.

Furthermore, MrBeast's friendships have opened doors

and created opportunities for collaboration with other popular creators. By leveraging his network, he has been able to feature guest appearances from some of the biggest names on YouTube, expanding his reach and introducing his content to new audiences.

Fiendship and support have been instrumental in MrBeast's journey to success. His inner circle, filled with close friends who have been there through thick and thin, has provided him with the support and inspiration needed to overcome challenges and create groundbreaking content. Additionally, his role models have shaped his perspective on success and guided him towards using his platform for the greater good. Through his friendships, MrBeast has not only found success but has also demonstrated the power of friendship in shaping one's path to greatness.

BEHIND EVERY GREAT YOUTUBER: MEET THE COLLABORATIVE FORCES

When you think of MrBeast, the first thing that probably comes to mind is his larger-than-life personality and jaw-dropping stunts. But what many people may not realize is that behind every great YouTuber, there is a dedicated and talented team working tirelessly behind the scenes. In this chapter, we will dive into the world of MrBeast and shed light on the collaborative forces that have propelled his phenomenal rise to success.

MrBeast, whose real name is Jimmy Donaldson, may be the face of his YouTube channel, but he is far from a one-man show. He is supported by a team of skilled individuals who help bring his vision to life. From video editors and graphic designers to social media managers and business strategists, each member plays a crucial role in the success of the channel. Together, they work seamlessly to create engaging content that captivates millions of viewers around the world.

Building a creative team requires careful consideration and a keen eye for talent. MrBeast handpicked each member of his team, ensuring that they not only possess the necessary skills but also share his passion and dedication. This cohesive unit functions like a well-oiled machine, constantly brainstorming new ideas, refining their craft, and pushing the boundaries of what is possible in the world of YouTube.

Collaboration has been a key element in MrBeast's rise to fame. He understands the power of joining forces with other YouTubers and influencers to create content that is both entertaining and impactful. By collaborating with like-minded individuals, MrBeast is able to tap into new audiences and expand his reach beyond his core fanbase.

These collaborations often take the form of challenges, where MrBeast and his fellow YouTubers compete against each other in various tasks. Not only do these challenges generate excitement and anticipation among their respective fanbases, but they also showcase the camaraderie and friendship that exists within the YouTube community.

MrBeast's influence extends far beyond the borders of the United States. He has successfully collaborated with international influencers from all corners of the globe, further solidifying his status as a global phenomenon. These collaborations not only introduce MrBeast to new audiences but also provide a platform for these international influencers to gain exposure to a wider fanbase.

From participating in challenges with popular European YouTubers to engaging in friendly competitions with Asian influencers, MrBeast's collaborations transcend language and cultural barriers. This international reach has not only boosted his subscriber count but has also cemented his position as a trailblazer in the world of YouTube.

One of the reasons why MrBeast's rise to success has been so meteoric is his ability to engage with his worldwide fanbase. He understands the importance of connecting with his viewers on a personal level and goes above and beyond to make them feel appreciated and valued.

Whether it's responding to comments, interacting with fans on social media, or organizing meet-ups and fan events, MrBeast is constantly finding new ways to show his appreciation. This level of engagement has not only fostered a strong sense of loyalty among his fanbase but has also attracted new fans who are drawn to his genuine and down-to-earth personality.

Building a winning team is no easy feat, but MrBeast has certainly cracked the code. If you aspire to create a successful YouTube channel or any venture for that matter, it is crucial to surround yourself with individuals who share your vision and complement your strengths.

The first step is to identify the specific skills and expertise you need on your team. From video editing and content creation to marketing and analytics, each role should be carefully considered. Once you have a clear idea of the roles you need to fill, it is important to thoroughly vet potential candidates, looking beyond their qualifications to assess their passion, work ethic, and ability to collaborate.

MrBeast's phenomenal rise to success is a testament to the power of collaboration and the importance of building a strong and dedicated team. Behind every great YouTuber, there are individuals who work tirelessly to bring their vision to life and engage with their fanbase. MrBeast's success story serves as an inspiration to aspiring content creators and entrepreneurs, reminding us that with the right team and a passion for what you do, anything is possible.

THE TRANSFORMATION OF CHRIS TYSON: FROM SOUTHERN GUN-LOVING DUDE TO TRANSGENDER ADVOCATE

C hris Tyson had always felt like something wasn't quite right. Growing up in the South, he was taught to love guns, beer, and football. He tried to fit in with the expectations of his community, but he always felt like he was pretending.

Then, one day, he found his sister's dresses in her closet. At first, he was curious, but then he felt something stir inside of him. He realized that he was experiencing gender dysphoria, and he didn't know what to do about it.

For years, Tyson struggled with his gender identity. He tried to ignore it, to push it away, but it always came back. Then, in November 2020, he came out as bisexual. It was a big step, but it wasn't enough. He still felt like he was living a lie.

Finally, after years of struggling, Tyson made a decision. He was going to start hormone replacement therapy (HRT). It wasn't an easy decision, but he knew it was the right one.

Tyson started HRT two months ago, and he says his physical appearance has already started to change. He credits his two-year-old son with helping him get through the treatment. His son has taught him so much about himself in such a short time, and Tyson is grateful for him every day.

Tyson understands that not everyone will support his decision to transition, but he hopes that by sharing his story, he can help others who are struggling with their own gender identity. He knows that the road ahead will be challenging, but he's ready for it.

In a world where gender non-conforming people have to jump through hoops to get life-saving gender-affirming healthcare, Tyson is an advocate for change. He hopes that one day, everyone will be able to access the care they need without fear of judgment or discrimination.

The transformation of Chris Tyson from a Southern gun-loving dude to a transgender advocate is a powerful reminder that it's never too late to be true to yourself.

CHRIS TYSON'S TRANSFORMATION: THE IMPACT ON MRBEAST'S BRAND

In the world of business, maintaining a brand image is crucial, and any deviation from that image can lead to disastrous consequences. Such is the case with the recent Chris Tyson situation, which has the potential to become a complete disaster for MrBeast's brand. However, it may also provide some unique benefits.

In mid-2022, fans began to notice that Chris Tyson, one of the main personalities of the MrBeast channel, was changing. Chris used to represent the quintessential Southern gun and truck-loving dude, but he began to display increasingly feminine traits, such as getting his nails done and changing his facial appearance. This led to criticism from some fans, who saw this transformation as a betrayal of the image Chris had built up over the years.

The true catalyst for Chris Tyson's feminization seemed to have come from his marriage, which ended in January 2022. Chris went from lighting campfires and raising a family with his beautiful wife to trying to be a wife with his man buds and long nails. As the criticism continued to pile up, Chris announced that he'd be taking a break from social media.

While there was a possibility that Chris would make efforts to return to his former self, he decided to double down on his feminine image. This decision received mixed reactions from MrBeast's co-workers and fans. Some saw it as a positive step forward for gender identity and praised Chris's courage in embracing his true self. Others criticized Chris for "ripping apart his family" and "depriving his son of a father figure."

As a brand, MrBeast must navigate this situation carefully. On the one hand, embracing Chris's transformation can send a powerful message of inclusivity and diversity. On the other hand, it may alienate some of the channel's core audience who may not be ready to accept such a radical departure from the image they've come to expect.

However, if handled correctly, MrBeast's brand could emerge from this situation stronger than ever. By embracing Chris's transformation and promoting a message of inclusivity and acceptance, MrBeast's brand could become a powerful force for positive change. At the same time, the controversy could attract new viewers who are looking for content that embraces diversity and challenges traditional gender roles.

In conclusion, the Chris Tyson situation has the potential to become a complete disaster for MrBeast's brand, but it may also provide some unique benefits. By embracing Chris's transformation and promoting a message of inclusivity and acceptance, MrBeast's brand could emerge from this situation stronger than ever. It remains to be seen how the situation will ultimately play out, but one thing is clear: MrBeast's brand will never be the same again.

THE POWER OF LAUGHTER: HOW MRBEAST'S PRANK WARS ARE REVOLUTIONIZING ONLINE ENTERTAINMENT

Content creators are constantly seeking new ways to captivate audiences and create viral sensations. One individual who has taken the digital realm by storm is MrBeast, a YouTube personality known for his extravagant pranks and philanthropic ventures. We will delve into the power of laughter and explore how MrBeast's prank wars have revolutionized online entertainment, captivating millions of viewers worldwide.

Humor has always been a fundamental aspect of entertainment, and its impact in the digital landscape cannot be underestimated. Laughter is contagious, and it has the power to forge connections between content creators and their audiences. MrBeast understands this concept and harnesses the power of laughter to engage viewers and keep them coming back for more.

One of the key reasons behind the success of MrBeast's prank wars is their ability to generate viral content. These pranks are carefully crafted to evoke genuine reactions, often combining shock, surprise, and hilarity. When viewers witness someone being pranked, they experience a range of emotions that they are eager to share with others. This sharing behavior is what fuels the viral nature of MrBeast's content, as viewers eagerly pass it along to their friends, family, and social media followers.

Prank videos tap into the innate human desire for amusement and surprise. They provide a temporary escape from the mundane and offer a sense of excitement and unpredictability. Additionally, prank videos often involve relatable situations, allowing viewers to imagine themselves in similar scenarios. This sense of identification draws viewers in and creates a deeper emotional connection with the content.

While MrBeast's prank wars may seem spontaneous and chaotic, there is a strategic approach behind them. Each prank is carefully planned and executed to maximize its impact. MrBeast understands the importance of timing, suspense, and surprise in creating compelling content. By strategically releasing his prank videos at the right moments, he ensures that they have the greatest chance of going viral and reaching a wide audience.

The success of MrBeast's prank wars extends beyond mere entertainment value. Brands and businesses have recognized the marketing potential of aligning themselves with MrBeast's content. Through clever product placements and sponsorships, companies can reach MrBeast's massive audience while benefiting from the positive association with laughter and fun. This mutually beneficial relationship allows MrBeast to continue creating high-quality content while generating revenue to support his philanthropic endeavors.

MrBeast's prank wars have undeniably revolutionized the landscape of online entertainment. They have set a new standard for creativity, production value, and audience engagement. Other content creators have taken note and begun incorporating pranks and practical jokes into their own videos. This shift has injected a fresh wave of excitement into the digital sphere, pushing the boundaries of what is considered entertaining and captivating.

While MrBeast's prank wars have garnered immense popularity, they also raise ethical considerations. Some argue that the stunts and pranks may cross the line of what is morally acceptable. It is essential for content creators to strike a balance between entertainment and respect for others' boundaries. MrBeast himself has acknowledged this responsibility and strives to ensure that his pranks do not cause harm or distress to anyone involved.

MrBeast is not the only content creator to embrace the world of prank wars. There are numerous influencers who have successfully incorporated pranks into their content, each with their own unique style and approach. From hidden camera pranks to elaborate practical jokes, these creators continue to captivate audiences with their humor and wit.

As online entertainment evolves, so too will the concept of prank wars. With advancements in technology and the ever-changing tastes of audiences, content creators will need to continually innovate and adapt to stay relevant. Prank wars will likely continue to entertain and engage viewers, but in new and unexpected ways. The future holds exciting possibilities for the evolution of this form of entertainment.

MrBeast's prank wars have undoubtedly left a lasting impact on online entertainment. Through his strategic approach, he has harnessed the power of laughter to create viral content and revolutionize the digital space. While ethical considerations remain, prank wars have become a staple of online entertainment, captivating audiences worldwide. As we look to the future, we eagerly await the next wave of creativity and innovation that will shape the landscape of prank wars in the digital

realm.

BEHIND THE CAMERA: UNVEILING THE UNSEEN OBSTACLES FACED BY MRBEAST ON HIS PATH TO STARDOM

As fans, we often see the glamorous side of our favorite content creators. We witness their incredible videos, their engaging personalities, and their rise to stardom. However, what we don't see are the unseen obstacles they face behind the camera. One such content creator who has worked tirelessly to establish himself in the digital space is MrBeast. In now, we will delve into the challenges he has encountered on his path to success.

One of the key elements that sets MrBeast's content apart is the extravagant nature of his videos. From giving away large sums of money to staging jaw-dropping challenges, his content is a spectacle to behold. However, what many of us fail to realize is the financial burden that comes with creating such videos. The cost of production, equipment, and props can easily run into the thousands, if not millions, of dollars.

To fund his ambitious projects, MrBeast has had to rely on sponsorships, brand deals, and merchandise sales. While these revenue streams have been instrumental in supporting his content creation, they also come with their own challenges. Securing sponsorships and brand deals requires constant negotiation and maintaining relationships with companies. Additionally, the pressure to constantly produce high-quality content that aligns with the expectations of sponsors can be overwhelming.

Creating content consistently is no easy feat, and it takes a toll on the mental and emotional well-being of content creators like MrBeast. The pressure to come up with new ideas, maintain engagement with the audience, and stay relevant in an ever-changing landscape can be exhausting. The need to constantly outdo oneself and push the boundaries of creativity can lead to burnout and mental fatigue.

Moreover, the online world can be a harsh and unforgiving place. Content creators often face criticism, hate, and negative comments from viewers. While MrBeast has cultivated a positive and supportive community, he is not immune to negativity. Dealing with constant scrutiny and criticism can be emotionally draining and can take a toll on one's self-esteem. It requires immense strength and resilience to stay focused and continue creating content in the face of such adversity.

Criticism is an inevitable part of being in the public eye, and MrBeast is no stranger to it. Despite his immense popularity and positive impact, he has still faced his fair share of negativity. Some viewers criticize his giving away of money, claiming it is wasteful or not truly altruistic. Others question the authenticity of his challenges and accuse him of staging his videos for entertainment purposes.

While it is impossible to please everyone, MrBeast has managed to address criticism in a mature and productive manner. He takes constructive feedback to heart and uses it to improve his content. Moreover, he understands that not everyone will understand or appreciate his vision, and he remains true to himself and his values. By focusing on the positive impact he can have on people's lives, MrBeast has been able to rise above the negativity and continue making a difference.

One aspect that is often overlooked is the challenge of balancing personal life and the online persona of content creators. MrBeast's rise to stardom has undoubtedly brought him fame and fortune, but it has also come at a cost. Maintaining a sense of privacy and normalcy in the midst of a highly publicized career is challenging. The constant scrutiny and invasion of personal space can take a toll on one's mental and emotional well-being.

However, MrBeast has managed to find a balance between his personal life and his online persona. He has surrounded himself with a supportive team that helps him navigate the challenges of fame. Additionally, he has created boundaries and designated time for himself and his loved ones, ensuring that he doesn't lose touch with what truly matters outside of his digital empire. This ability to maintain perspective and prioritize personal well-being is essential for long-term success and happiness.

The unseen obstacles faced by MrBeast on his path to stardom are a testament to his determination and resilience. From the financial burdens of creating extravagant videos to the mental and emotional toll of constant content creation, MrBeast has faced numerous challenges. Yet, he has managed to overcome them by staying true to himself, addressing criticism constructively, and finding a balance between his personal and online life. As fans, we should appreciate the effort and dedication it takes to create the content we love and support our favorite creators on their journey to success.

LEARNING FROM MRBEAST'S BACKLASHES

Avoiding Common Mistakes
in the Digital Age

In the world of the digital age, it is not uncommon for individuals and brands to face backlashes due to the online content they produce. One such example is MrBeast, a popular YouTuber known for his extravagant and often charitable stunts. Despite his massive success, MrBeast has also experienced his fair share of backlashes throughout his career. These backlashes serve as valuable lessons for content creators, highlighting the importance of being mindful and avoiding common mistakes in the digital age.

Learning from mistakes is an essential part of personal and professional growth. In the digital age, where information spreads rapidly and opinions can be shared instantaneously, it is crucial to take any setback as an opportunity to learn and improve. Backlashes can have a significant impact on an individual or brand's reputation, potentially leading to loss of followers, customers, and even business opportunities. However, by analyzing and understanding the mistakes made, one can navigate the digital landscape more effectively and avoid similar pitfalls in the future.

The digital age has brought about new challenges and opportunities for content creators. With the power to reach a global audience, it is essential to be aware of common mistakes that can lead to backlashes. One common mistake is a lack of thorough research and understanding of the target audience. It is crucial to know who you are creating content for and what their expectations and values are. Ignorance or insensitivity towards cultural, social, or political issues can result in severe backlash.

Another common mistake is the misuse of social media platforms. It is easy to get caught up in the quest for attention and engagement, but it is important to remember that every action has consequences. Posting offensive or controversial content without considering the potential impact can lead to significant repercussions. Additionally, excessive self-promotion and lack of authenticity can also lead to negative reactions from the audience.

MrBeast, with his philanthropic and extravagant

content, has amassed a massive following on YouTube. However, even he has faced backlashes throughout his career. One notable case was when he organized a viral challenge that involved planting trees. While the initiative was well-intentioned, there were concerns raised about the environmental impact of the project. Critics argued that the mass planting of trees without proper planning and consideration for the ecosystem could potentially do more harm than good. This incident serves as a reminder that good intentions alone are not enough. Thorough research and consultation with experts are necessary to avoid unintended consequences.

Another instance of backlash against MrBeast occurred when he organized a challenge where participants were required to stay in a glass box suspended in the air. This challenge received backlash due to concerns regarding safety and the potential for participants to suffer from anxiety or panic attacks. It highlighted the importance of prioritizing the well-being and safety of individuals involved in content creation. Being mindful of the potential risks and ensuring adequate precautions are in place can help mitigate the chances of facing such backlashes.

Despite the backlashes MrBeast has faced, his brand remains strong and continues to thrive. This can be attributed to his ability to handle the situations with grace and transparency. MrBeast acknowledged the concerns raised by his audience, addressed them openly, and took steps to rectify the situation. By listening to his audience and showing a willingness to learn from his mistakes, he was able to regain trust and maintain the loyalty of his followers. This emphasizes the importance of humility and accountability when facing backlashes in the digital age.

This have provided valuable lessons for content creators. One of the key takeaways is the importance of being well-informed and conducting thorough research before embarking on any project. Understanding the potential impact and consequences of your content can help you avoid unintended backlashes. Additionally, it is crucial to prioritize the well-being and safety of individuals involved in content creation. Striking a balance between creating engaging content and ensuring the welfare of participants is vital for building a positive reputation.

To avoid common mistakes in the digital age, content creators should adopt certain strategies. Firstly, it is essential to know your audience and their expectations. Conducting audience research and staying informed about the latest trends and issues will enable you to create content that resonates with your target demographic. Secondly, transparency and authenticity are paramount. Building trust with your audience by being genuine and honest in your content will help establish a loyal following. Lastly, embracing a proactive approach and being open to feedback will allow you to learn and grow from any mistakes you may make along the way.

Best Practices for Managing Online Reputation

Maintaining a positive online reputation is crucial in the digital age. To do so, content creators should adhere to best practices for managing their online presence. Firstly, it is important to monitor and respond to comments and feedback promptly. Engaging with your audience and addressing any concerns or criticisms shows that you value their opinions and are willing to listen. Secondly, it is essential to stay consistent with your brand image and values. Inconsistencies or contradicting messages can lead to confusion and potential backlashes. Lastly, being mindful of the content you share and the potential impact it may have is vital for maintaining a positive online reputation.

Transparency and authenticity play a significant role in avoiding backlashes in the digital age. Being transparent about your intentions, motivations, and processes helps build trust with your audience. It shows that you have nothing to hide and are genuinely invested in creating valuable content. Authenticity, on the other hand, involves staying true to yourself and your values. Trying to please everyone or conforming to popular opinions can lead to inauthentic content that may not resonate with your audience. By being transparent and authentic, you can mitigate the chances of facing backlashes.

Content creators must embrace a proactive approach. This involves staying informed about current trends, issues, and potential controversies. By being proactive, content creators can anticipate and address any concerns or criticisms before they escalate into full-blown backlashes. Additionally, actively seeking feedback from your audience and continuously improving your content based on their input can help you stay ahead of potential pitfalls. Embracing a proactive approach demonstrates your commitment to growth and improvement, ultimately minimizing the chances of facing backlashes.

Learning from mistakes is essential in the digital age, where backlashes can have a significant impact on an individual or brand's reputation. By analyzing the mistakes made by content creators like MrBeast, we can avoid similar pitfalls and navigate the digital landscape more effectively. Strategies such as thorough research, prioritizing safety and well-being, transparency, authenticity, and a proactive approach can help content creators avoid common mistakes and manage their online reputation successfully. By learning from MrBeast's backlashes and implementing these strategies, we can create content that resonates with our audience while avoiding unnecessary controversies.

DISCOVER HOW MRBEAST MASTERED NICHE SELECTION

Youtube has revolutionized the way we consume video content, providing a platform for creators to showcase their talent, share their knowledge, and build a dedicated audience. With over 2 billion monthly active users, YouTube presents an incredible opportunity for individuals and businesses alike to reach a global audience. However, with such a vast array of content available, standing out from the crowd and achieving YouTube success can be a daunting task. One of the key factors that can make or break your YouTube journey is niche selection.

Niche selection refers to the process of identifying a specific topic or theme for your YouTube channel. Instead of trying to cover a wide range of subjects, focusing on a niche allows you to establish yourself as an authority in a particular area. This not only helps you attract a dedicated audience but also makes it easier for

YouTube's algorithm to recommend your videos to those who are interested in your niche.

Choosing the right niche is crucial for your YouTube success for several reasons. Firstly, it helps you define your target audience. By catering to a specific group of people with shared interests, you can tailor your content to meet their needs and preferences. This leads to higher engagement and viewer retention, as your audience feels a connection and relevance to your videos.

Secondly, niche selection allows you to differentiate yourself from the competition. With millions of YouTube channels vying for attention, finding a unique angle within your chosen niche helps you stand out and attract viewers who are looking for a fresh perspective. By providing valuable and unique content, you can establish yourself as an authority in your niche and build a loyal following.

Case study: MrBeast's journey to YouTube success

To understand the power of niche selection, let's take a look at the inspiring journey of MrBeast a YouTube creator who has achieved remarkable success through his strategic niche selection. MrBeast started his YouTube channel with a passion for technology and gadgets, but he quickly realized that the tech niche was highly saturated. Instead of giving up, he decided to narrow down his focus and delve deeper into a specific aspect of technology – smartphone reviews for budget-conscious consumers.

Mrbeast's success story began with careful analysis and research. He studied the YouTube landscape, identified popular niches, and evaluated the level of competition within each one. After analyzing the data, he discovered that there was a significant demand for smartphone reviews targeting budget-conscious consumers. This niche had a dedicated audience hungry for information and advice on affordable smartphones.

Finding the perfect niche for your YouTube channel requires a combination of research, self-reflection, and creativity. Here are some strategies to help you identify a niche that aligns with your interests and has the potential for success:

Explore your passions:
Start by making a list of topics or subjects that genuinely interest you. This could be anything from fitness and cooking to travel and fashion. Your enthusiasm for the niche will shine through in your content and resonate with your audience.

Research market demand:
Use tools like Google Trends, keyword research tools, and social media platforms to gauge the popularity and demand for different niches. Look for areas where there is a growing interest but relatively less competition.

Analyze the competition:

Study the top channels within your chosen niche and analyze their content, engagement levels, and audience demographics. This will help you identify gaps in the market and find a unique angle to differentiate yourself.

Consider your expertise:
Assess your knowledge and expertise in different areas. Choosing a niche where you have experience and can provide valuable insights will not only make your content more authentic but also help you establish credibility and authority.

Once you have identified a potential niche, it's essential to evaluate the level of competition within that space. While some competition is healthy, an oversaturated niche can make it challenging to stand out.

Here are some key factors to consider when evaluating competition:

Number of channels:
Look at the number of channels already covering your chosen niche. If there are too many established channels, it might be difficult to gain visibility and attract an audience.

Quality of content:
Assess the quality of content produced by existing channels. Identify their strengths and weaknesses, and strive to offer something unique and valuable to your audience.

Engagement levels:

Analyze the engagement levels of top channels within your niche. Look at the number of views, likes, comments, and shares their videos receive. This will give you an idea of the type of content that resonates with the audience and help you tailor your own content strategy. Once you have chosen your niche and evaluated the competition, it's time to develop a content strategy that aligns with your niche and audience. Here are some tips to help you create compelling and engaging content:

Identify your target audience:

Understand your audience's demographics, interests, and preferences. This will help you create content that resonates with them and keeps them coming back for more.

Plan your content calendar:

Consistency is key on YouTube. Create a content calendar that outlines the topics, formats, and release schedule for your videos. This will help you stay organized and ensure a steady stream of content for your audience.

Diversify your content:

Experiment with different formats, such as tutorials, reviews, interviews, and vlogs, to cater to different preferences within your niche. This will keep your content fresh and engaging.

Listen to your audience:

Pay attention to comments, messages, and feedback from your viewers. This will give you valuable insights into what they want to see more of and help you refine your content strategy.

Building a dedicated audience within your niche takes time and effort. Here are some tips to help you grow and engage your audience:

Engage with your viewers:
Respond to comments, messages, and questions from your viewers. This shows that you value their input and creates a sense of community around your channel.

Collaborate with other creators:
Collaborating with other YouTubers in your niche can expose your channel to a new audience and help you build credibility. Look for opportunities to collaborate on videos or cross-promote each other's content.

Promote your channel:
Leverage social media platforms, forums, and online communities to promote your YouTube channel. Engage in relevant discussions and share your content where appropriate, but make sure to follow community guidelines and avoid spamming.

Optimize your video SEO:
Use relevant keywords, tags, and descriptions to optimize your videos for search engines and YouTube's

algorithm. This will increase the visibility of your content and attract organic traffic to your channel.

Choosing the right niche not only helps you build a loyal audience but also opens up opportunities for monetization. Here are some benefits of niche selection for YouTube monetization:

Targeted advertising:
By catering to a specific niche, you attract advertisers who are interested in reaching your audience. This leads to higher-quality ads and increased revenue potential.

Sponsorship opportunities:
As you establish yourself as an authority in your niche, you may attract sponsorship opportunities from brands and companies looking to collaborate with influencers in your space.

Product recommendations and affiliate marketing:
When you have a dedicated audience interested in a specific niche, you can recommend relevant products and earn a commission through affiliate marketing. This can be a significant source of passive income.

Merchandise and merchandise collaboration:
Niche selection allows you to create merchandise that resonates with your audience. From t-shirts to mugs, you can leverage your niche to design and sell merchandise that your viewers will love.

Niche selection is a critical step in cracking the code to YouTube success. By identifying a specific niche, understanding your audience, and developing a content strategy that aligns with their needs, you can build a dedicated following and unlock the monetization potential of YouTube. Remember, finding the perfect niche requires research, creativity, and a genuine passion for your topic. So go ahead, explore your passions, analyze the competition, and embark on your journey to YouTube success.

MARKETING LESSONS FROM MRBEAST

Embrace Innovation:

YouTube is flooded with videos that are often just copies of something that's already been done before. While this formula may work, it's important to strive for innovation and create something truly unique. To achieve this, you should always experiment and differentiate yourself by creating new formats.

For example, MrBeast never stops trying new things. He's known for creating new formats that blend multiple genres, and has even managed to plant 20 million trees through one of his most impressive challenges. However, innovation doesn't come easy, and for years Jimmy produced hundreds of videos that never worked. Patience and self-assessment are crucial when it comes to building a strong bond with your audience.

Follow Trends:

While innovation is important, it's also essential to keep up with the latest trends in order to stay relevant. However, this doesn't mean you should copy what everyone else is doing. Instead, you should use your creativity and adapt the trends to your own unique style.

MrBeast is a master at riding trends. He has a way of shifting the focus of his channel masterfully from himself and finding a way to ride every popping trend that's out there. He has also used bigger names to his advantage by donating absurd amounts on streams or doing free advertisements for other channels. For instance, during last year's SuperBowl, he managed to do a free advertisement for the biggest YouTuber at that time with his friends.

Invest In Your Channel:

To maintain momentum and growth on your channel, it's important to invest accordingly. This means dedicating time, effort, and even resources to nurturing and growing your channel.

MrBeast has always understood the importance of investing in his channel. He has affirmed more than once that all of his revenues, until recently, were invested in videos. You don't need to invest everything in your channel like he does, but you can create a scaling plan that fits your goals to help you out.

Show Kindness:

Kindness and empathy are winning business strategies, and MrBeast is a living example of this. His channel is based on expensive stunts and good deeds, which has been his long-term winning strategy. People never get bored with the guy as he offers ridiculous amounts of gifts and cash to people and tries to change people's lives for the better.

One of his videos, for instance, is named "I Ordered a Pizza and Tipped the House." And it is exactly as it sounds: they offered a new house to the pizza delivery guy that first came. When you put your audience at the center of your interests and offer kindness and generosity, people will naturally gravitate towards you.

Add Shock Value:

People crave extraordinary stories, and they want to see something that's never been done before. This is where shock value comes into play. Your video titles and thumbnails should be crafted in a way that makes users curious and excited to see what will happen next.

MrBeast is a master of clickbait, and he uses many techniques to keep his viewers engaged until the very end. This includes creative intros, hooks, and other challenges inside the video, as well as showcasing his friends' vlogs or POV's. He also offers giveaways, which not only attract new viewers but also keep his current audience hooked.

UNLOCKING MRBEAST'S VIRAL FORMULA

The thing is, Mr Beast has tapped into the power of effective messaging.

For communication to cut through the noise and be effective, generally it must possess one or several of these elements:

- Expense
- Absurdity

- Illogicality
- Extravagance
- Scarcity
- Humour

And that's the fuel behind almost all of his videos.

Here are the titles of Mr Beast's most popular videos:

- $456,000 Squid Game In Real Life!
- Last To Leave Circle Wins $500,000
- I Spent 50 Hours In Solitary Confinement
- Press This Button To Win $100,000!
- Anything You Can Fit In The Circle I'll Pay For
- Would You Sit In Snakes For $10,000?
- I Ate A $70,000 Golden Pizza
- Last To Leave $800,000 Island Keeps It
- $1 vs $1,000,000 Hotel Room!

But what's the secret in it? I can ask ChatGPT to create

it???

The thing that grabs the attention of the viewer is that every title and video subject makes, these titles are wrapped around a series of core frameworks he seems to use all of the time.

1. High Stakes Content

- "Last to leave $800,000 Island keeps it"
- "Last to fall wins $100,000 dollars"

2. Giving Content

- "I broke into a house and left $50,000"
- "Giving 10,000 Presents to Kids for Christmas"

3. Survival Content

- "Surviving 24 Hours Straight In A Desert"
- "Surviving 24 Hours Straight In A Rainforest"

4. "I Did" Content

- "I Spent $30,000 On Lottery Tickets And Won"
- "I Ate $100,000 Golden Ice Cream"

But there's more to this than just titling these videos create a cycle of continued viewership, and it's all around the type of content he creates.

Here are five things to do for creating successful content and attracting a loyal audience.

1. Creating content that resonates with your audience
2. being authentic and transparent
3. being consistent in quality and frequency of posts
4. experimenting and taking risks, building a community of fans
5. collaborating with others in your industry are some of these strategies.

Using these strategies, Mr. Beast has built his brand and achieved success on YouTube, and they can be applied by businesses and content creators to create engaging content, build loyal followings, and succeed in the long run.

FEASTABLES: THE JOURNEY OF MRBEAST'S BRAND INTO THE WORLD OF FOOD

In recent years, social media has revolutionized the way we consume content. From fashion to travel, influencers have taken over various industries, and the food industry is no exception. These influencers have the power to shape trends, influence consumer behavior, and even launch their own brands. One such influencer who has made a significant impact on the food industry is MrBeast.

MrBeast, known for his philanthropic acts and attention-grabbing challenges, has expanded his brand into the world of food. With millions of followers across platforms like YouTube and Instagram, he has leveraged his massive audience to create unique and engaging food-related content. From massive food challenges to showcasing the best local eats, MrBeast has become a trusted source for food enthusiasts around the globe.

MrBeast's food-related content has gained immense popularity, attracting millions of views and engagements. His unique approach to creating content that appeals to both food lovers and thrill-seekers has set him apart from other influencers in the industry. Each video is meticulously crafted to captivate the audience's attention, combining mouth-watering visuals with exciting challenges that keep viewers on the edge of their seats.

One of MrBeast's most well-known food challenges was the "World's Largest Pizza" challenge. In this video, he collaborated with a local pizzeria to create a massive pizza that broke records. The video garnered millions of views and sparked a viral trend of food challenges across social media platforms. This success not only solidified MrBeast's position as a prominent figure in the food industry but also showcased his ability to create content that resonates with a wide audience.

Beyond creating entertaining content, MrBeast has used his influence to make a positive impact on communities through food-related philanthropic initiatives. One such initiative was his "Feeding the Homeless" challenge, where he personally distributed meals to those in need. This act of kindness not only showcased MrBeast's generosity but also inspired his followers to get involved in similar charitable endeavors.

In addition to direct acts of charity, MrBeast has also collaborated with various food brands to raise money for charitable causes. For example, he partnered with a popular fast-food chain to create a limited-edition menu item, with a portion of the proceeds donated to a children's charity. These collaborations not only generate funds for worthy causes but also raise awareness among MrBeast's massive audience.

MrBeast's brand has had a profound impact on the food industry, influencing consumer behavior and shaping trends. His food challenges and recommendations have the power to turn lesser-known local eateries into overnight sensations. By featuring small businesses in his videos, MrBeast has helped these establishments gain exposure and attract new customers, ultimately boosting their revenue and success.

Furthermore, MrBeast's influence has extended beyond traditional media platforms. He has ventured into the world of branded merchandise, releasing a line of food-related products that his followers eagerly purchase. This demonstrates the power of his brand and the trust his audience has in his recommendations. By leveraging his influence and expanding his brand, MrBeast has created a unique and profitable business model within the food industry.

As MrBeast continues to innovate and expand his brand, his legacy in the world of food is undeniable.

He has not only entertained millions with his food-related content but has also made a meaningful impact through his philanthropic efforts. MrBeast has shown that influencers can use their platform to bring about positive change and inspire others to do the same.

MrBeast's journey into the world of food has been nothing short of extraordinary. From his foray into the industry to the success of his food-related content, he has captured the attention and admiration of millions. Through his philanthropic initiatives and impact on the food industry, MrBeast has left a lasting legacy that will continue to shape the future of food content creation and influence consumer behavior.

MRBEAST CHANGING THE FACE OF YOUTUBE AND BEYOND

MrBeast has left an indelible mark on both the YouTube community and the wider world, thanks to his daring stunts and philanthropic endeavors. He serves as a shining example and role model to millions of fans all over the world.

One of the hallmarks of MrBeast's success has been his willingness to push the envelope and explore various forms of content. He has blazed new trails and established fresh video styles and formats, from his "24 Hour" challenges to his "Last to Leave" competitions. His creative pursuits have sparked creativity in numerous other creators, who have been inspired to emulate his example and innovate in their own unique ways.

But MrBeast's contributions extend beyond just entertaining content. He has also leveraged his platform to promote awareness and funding for important causes. He has spearheaded several highly successful campaigns to benefit charities such as St. Jude Children's Research Hospital and Team Trees, which aimed to plant 20 million trees by 2020. Through these efforts, he has demonstrated a remarkable commitment to using his fame and influence for the greater good.

Beyond YouTube, MrBeast has had a significant impact on popular culture and the broader media landscape. He has been featured in numerous news articles and television segments, and has even been named one of Time Magazine's 100 most influential people.

MrBeast's impact on the world of content creation extends far beyond his own channel and his immediate fanbase. His success story has become an inspiration for a new generation of creators who are looking to follow in his footsteps and make their mark on the world.

By showcasing the power of hard work, determination, and a willingness to take risks and experiment, MrBeast has provided a blueprint for success that has resonated with millions of young people around the world. His story is a testament to the fact that anyone can achieve greatness if they are willing to put in the time and effort required.

Looking to the future, MrBeast remains focused on expanding his brand and using his platform to make a positive impact on the world. He has proven time and time again that he is not afraid to take on big challenges and push himself creatively, and his fans eagerly await each new video and philanthropic campaign. As MrBeast continues to grow and evolve as a creator, his impact on the world is sure to continue growing as well.

HOW PHILANTHROPY SHAPED MRBEAST'S JOURNEY

P hilanthropy is a powerful force that can transform lives and inspire greatness. In the case of MrBeast, it has been the driving force behind his extraordinary journey of philanthropy. Known for his record-breaking challenges and acts of generosity, MrBeast has captured the hearts of millions and become a symbol of hope and inspiration. We will delve into the early philanthropic efforts of MrBeast, explore his record-breaking challenges, examine the impact of his philanthropy on his brand, and uncover the valuable lessons we can learn from his journey. Let's embark on this incredible journey of generosity and greatness.

MrBeast's journey of philanthropy began long before he gained fame and fortune. Even in his early days as a content creator on YouTube, he showed a remarkable inclination towards helping others. He started by donating a portion of his earnings to various charities, raising awareness about important social issues, and encouraging his followers to make a difference. It was during this time that MrBeast realized the power of his platform and the potential he had to make a significant impact on the world.

As his channel grew in popularity, so did his philanthropic efforts. He started organizing small-scale challenges and fundraisers to raise money for causes close to his heart. From planting trees to feeding the homeless, MrBeast's early philanthropy laid the foundation for the larger-scale challenges that would later define his journey.

MrBeast's philanthropic journey took a monumental turn when he began organizing record-breaking challenges that pushed the boundaries of generosity. From giving away a million dollars to strangers to hosting the world's largest virtual rock-paper-scissors tournament, MrBeast's challenges captured the attention of millions and set new records in the realm of philanthropy. Each challenge was meticulously planned and executed, with the sole purpose of making a positive impact on the lives of others.

These challenges not only showcased MrBeast's creativity and determination but also highlighted the generosity of his sponsors and supporters. Through collaborations with brands and fellow YouTubers, MrBeast was able to amplify the impact of his philanthropy and reach a wider audience. His challenges became a source of inspiration for others, encouraging them to think outside the box and find innovative ways to give back to their communities.

MrBeast's philanthropy has had a profound impact on his personal brand. By using his platform to make a difference, he has built a loyal and engaged audience that sees him not just as a content creator, but as a philanthropist with a genuine desire to change the world. His acts of generosity have earned him respect and admiration from both his peers and his followers, solidifying his position as a prominent figure in the online community.

Additionally, MrBeast's philanthropy has opened doors for him to collaborate with other creators and brands that share his passion for giving back. Through these collaborations, he has been able to expand his reach and make an even greater impact on the causes he cares about. The positive association between MrBeast and philanthropy has become a key element of his brand identity, setting him apart from other content creators and making him a role model for aspiring philanthropists.

MrBeast's journey of philanthropy is not just a remarkable story, but also a source of valuable lessons for all of us. One of the most important lessons we can learn from him is the power of using our platforms and resources to make a positive impact. MrBeast's success as a philanthropist is a testament to the fact that anyone, regardless of their background or means, can make a difference in the world.

Another lesson we can learn from MrBeast is the importance of thinking big and taking risks. His record-breaking challenges were not only ambitious but also required a great deal of planning and coordination. By pushing the boundaries of what is possible, MrBeast has shown us that extraordinary acts of generosity can lead to extraordinary results.

Finally, MrBeast's journey teaches us the significance

of authenticity and transparency in philanthropy. Throughout his philanthropic endeavors, he has been open about his intentions, the impact of his donations, and the process behind his challenges. This level of transparency has not only earned him the trust of his audience but also ensured that his philanthropy is making a genuine and lasting impact.

As MrBeast's journey of philanthropy continues, the possibilities for his future endeavors are limitless. With each challenge, he raises the bar and sets new records, inspiring others to follow in his footsteps. It is likely that we will see more innovative and impactful challenges from MrBeast in the years to come, as he continues to use his platform for the greater good.

Moreover, MrBeast's influence extends beyond his own philanthropic efforts. By inspiring others to give back, he is creating a ripple effect of generosity that has the potential to change countless lives. As more creators and individuals join the movement, the impact of MrBeast's philanthropy will only grow stronger.

In the realm of philanthropy, MrBeast has carved a legacy of generosity and greatness. His journey from a small content creator to a global philanthropist is a testament to the power of giving back and the impact it can have on both individuals and communities. MrBeast has shown us that through acts of kindness and generosity, we can make a lasting difference in the world.

As we reflect on MrBeast's journey of philanthropy, let us be inspired to embrace the power of generosity in our own lives. Whether it is through small acts of kindness or larger-scale endeavors, we all have the ability to make a positive impact. Let us follow in the footsteps of MrBeast and strive for greatness through philanthropy.

Join the movement. Be a force for good. Together, we can

make a difference.

THE FUTURE OF MRBEAST ENTREPRENEURSHIP

MrBeast's foray into entrepreneurship through his online merchandise store is a testament to his business acumen and ability to capitalize on his brand's popularity. By diversifying his revenue streams beyond YouTube ad revenue, he has built a sustainable business that enables him to fund his ambitious philanthropic efforts.

Moreover, MrBeast's merchandise store serves as a powerful marketing tool that extends his brand's reach beyond YouTube. Fans can proudly wear his branded clothing and accessories, effectively becoming walking advertisements for his brand. This not only generates additional revenue but also strengthens the sense of community and loyalty among his fan base.

Through his ventures into entrepreneurship and philanthropy, MrBeast has shown that he is more than just a YouTube star; he is a multifaceted entrepreneur with a strong vision for the future. As he continues to expand his reach and impact, there is no doubt that MrBeast will continue to inspire and change the world in positive ways.

MrBeast's Finger on the App app is a prime example of his entrepreneurial spirit and his commitment to using his platform for good. The app not only provides users with an entertaining challenge, but also raises awareness and funds for important causes.

In fact, the app's first iteration, which launched in June 2020, aimed to support small businesses affected by the COVID-19 pandemic. Users who successfully kept their finger on the app for the longest time won a share of a $100,000 prize pool, while MrBeast and his team donated an additional $100,000 to small businesses struggling during the pandemic.

The app's second iteration, which launched in February 2021, aimed to raise awareness and funds for mental health. The cash prize was again set at $100,000, but this time users were encouraged to donate a portion of their winnings to mental health charities.

Overall, the Finger on the App app is just one of many ways in which MrBeast is using his platform and entrepreneurial skills to make a positive impact on the world. His success as a creator, entrepreneur, and philanthropist continues to inspire and motivate people around the globe.

Beyond his entrepreneurial ventures, MrBeast has also

continued to use his platform to raise awareness and funds for important causes. He has launched several new philanthropic campaigns, including a recent effort to provide clean drinking water to people in need around the world.

As MrBeast's brand and influence continue to expand, his vision for the future remains bold and ambitious. He has hinted at the possibility of launching new businesses and philanthropic ventures, all with the goal of making a positive impact on the world.

MrBeast has shown time and time again that he is not afraid to push boundaries and take risks, whether it's through his viral stunts or his innovative business ventures. His commitment to hard work, determination, and a desire to make a difference has earned him the respect and admiration of millions of fans around the world.

Despite his enormous success, MrBeast remains humble and focused on his core values. He understands the responsibility that comes with his platform and remains committed to using it for good. As he continues to blaze a trail in the world of entrepreneurship and philanthropy, there is no doubt that his impact on popular culture and the broader media landscape will only continue to grow.

LESSONS LEARNED FROM MRBEAST'S SUCCESS

MrBeast's willingness to experiment and take risks is rooted in his openness to experience, a personality trait that is associated with creativity, curiosity, and a desire for novelty.

Research has shown that individuals who score high in openness tend to be more flexible in their thinking, more willing to take risks, and more likely to pursue unconventional paths to success. MrBeast's openness likely helped him to identify new opportunities and approaches, and to adapt to changing circumstances as his career progressed.

This mindset is characterized by a belief that one's abilities and skills can be developed through hard work and perseverance, rather than being fixed traits that cannot be changed. Individuals with a growth mindset tend to be more resilient in the face of setbacks and challenges, and are more likely to view failure as an opportunity for learning and growth. MrBeast's commitment to hard work and determination, even in the face of challenges and failures, suggests that he has a growth mindset and a belief in the power of effort and persistence.

This success also highlights the importance of purpose and meaning in one's work. Research has shown that individuals who have a sense of purpose and meaning in their careers tend to be more satisfied, engaged, and successful. By using his platform to raise awareness and funds for important causes, MrBeast has found a sense of purpose and meaning in his work that likely contributes to his motivation and drive for success.

Focus on building a loyal audience. MrBeast's success on YouTube has been built on the foundation of a loyal and engaged audience. By consistently producing high-quality content that resonates with his fans, he has been able to grow his following and turn it into a powerful force for good.

Use your platform for good. MrBeast's philanthropic efforts have been a major driver of his success and a key reason why he has become such an inspiration to millions of fans around the world. By using his platform to raise awareness and funds for important causes, he has been able to make a positive impact on the world and build a strong sense of purpose around his brand.

Be authentic and true to yourself. MrBeast's success is also a testament to the power of authenticity. He has built his brand around his unique personality and approach to content creation, and his fans love him for it. By staying true to himself and his values, he has been able to build a strong and lasting connection with his audience.

Stay humble and committed to your goals. Despite his massive success, MrBeast remains grounded and committed to his core values. He has never lost sight of his desire to make a positive impact on the world, and he continues to work tirelessly towards that goal.

These are just a few of the lessons that can be learned from MrBeast's story. By embracing these principles and putting in the hard work required to achieve success, anyone can follow in his footsteps and build a career that makes a positive impact on the world.

THE IMPACT OF MRBEAST'S SUCCESS ON THE YOUTUBE LANDSCAPE

MrBeast's success on YouTube has had a significant impact on the broader media landscape and the content creation industry as a whole. Here are just a few of the ways in which his success has reshaped the YouTube landscape:

Increased competition: MrBeast's success has inspired countless other creators to try their hand at creating viral content and building large audiences on the platform. This has led to increased competition and a more diverse range of content on YouTube.

Emphasis on philanthropy:

MrBeast's philanthropic efforts have been a major source of inspiration for other creators on the platform, many of whom have launched their own charitable campaigns in response. This has helped to create a culture of giving and social responsibility among content creators on YouTube.

Changes in advertising and sponsorships:

MrBeast's massive reach and influence have made him an attractive partner for advertisers and sponsors, who are willing to pay top dollar to be associated with his brand. This has led to changes in the way that advertising and sponsorships are approached on the platform, with more emphasis on working with high-profile creators who have established themselves as leaders in their respective niches.

Greater scrutiny and regulation:

As YouTube has become more popular and influential, it has also come under greater scrutiny from regulators and lawmakers. MrBeast's success has brought increased attention to the platform, which has led to greater pressure to regulate and monitor the content that is being produced and shared on the site.

Evolution of content:

MrBeast's success has also had a direct impact on the types of content that are popular on YouTube. His focus on challenges, stunts, and other high-energy content has inspired countless other creators to try their hand at creating similar content, which has led to a proliferation of "challenge" videos and other viral content on the platform.

These are just a few of the ways in which MrBeast's success has impacted the YouTube landscape. As his influence continues to grow, it is likely that we will see even more changes in the way that content is created, shared, and monetized on the platform.

THE NEXT CHAPTER OF MRBEAST

As MrBeast's success continues to grow, many are left wondering what the future holds for his career and brand. Here are some of the key trends and factors that are likely to shape the next chapter of his story:

Expansion into new areas:

MrBeast has already expanded his brand beyond YouTube, with a popular podcast and a growing presence on other social media platforms. In the future, it is likely that we will see him continue to explore new avenues for growth, potentially including ventures into traditional media or even politics.

Continued emphasis on philanthropy:

MrBeast's philanthropic efforts have become a key part of his brand and a major source of inspiration for his fans. It is likely that we will see him continue to prioritize social impact and use his platform to raise awareness and funds for important causes.

Partnership with other creators:

MrBeast has already collaborated with many other high-profile creators on the platform, and this trend is likely to continue as he seeks out new ways to expand his reach and influence. We may see him work more closely with other philanthropic creators or influencers who share his values and approach to content creation.

Diversification of content:

While MrBeast is best known for his stunts, challenges, and other high-energy content, he has also shown an interest in exploring other types of content, such as documentaries and interviews. It is likely that we will see him continue to diversify his content in the future, potentially branching out into new genres or formats.

Maintaining authenticity:

Throughout his career, MrBeast has remained true to himself and his values, and this has been a major driver of his success. It is likely that he will continue to prioritize authenticity and transparency, even as he expands his brand and reaches new audiences.

These are just a few of the trends and factors that are likely to shape the future of MrBeast's career and brand. As he continues to grow and evolve, it is clear that he will remain a major force in the content creation industry and a source of inspiration for millions of fans around the world.

THE GOLDEN IDEAS FROM MRBEAST'S STORY

Mrbeast's rise to success is a testament to the power of hard work, dedication, and attention to detail. Throughout his career, he has demonstrated an unwavering commitment to providing his audience with the highest quality content possible, and this has paid off in a big way.

One of the key lessons we can learn from MrBeast's story is the importance of paying attention to the details. From the lighting and camera angles in his videos to the design and layout of his merchandise store, every aspect of his brand has been carefully crafted and executed to perfection.

This level of attention to detail can be seen in the way he approaches his content creation as well. He spends countless hours researching and planning each video, ensuring that every aspect of it is tailored to his audience's interests and preferences.

Another lesson we can learn from MrBeast is the importance of diversifying your revenue streams. While YouTube ad revenue is undoubtedly a significant part of his income, he has also built a thriving merchandise business, launched a popular podcast, and even started his own philanthropic organization.

By diversifying his revenue streams, MrBeast has been able to create a sustainable business model that isn't solely reliant on one source of income. This approach has helped him weather changes in the YouTube algorithm and other external factors that could potentially impact his earnings.

Here are just a few of the key takeaways from his success story:

Embrace failure:

MrBeast has been open about the fact that many of his early videos and stunts failed to gain traction. However, he didn't let those setbacks discourage him. Instead, he learned from his mistakes and kept trying new things until he found the formula that worked for him. Embracing failure is a key part of any entrepreneurial journey, and MrBeast's story is a testament to the importance of persistence in the face of adversity.

Focus on creating value:

MrBeast's success is built on the foundation of creating content that his audience finds valuable and entertaining. He has a deep understanding of what his fans want to see, and he works tirelessly to deliver on that promise. This focus on creating value for his audience has been a major driver of his success and is a valuable lesson for anyone looking to build a successful brand or business.

Build a strong team:

MrBeast has surrounded himself with a team of talented collaborators and advisors who have helped him to grow and scale his brand. He understands the importance of delegating responsibilities and working with others who share his vision and values. Building a strong team is crucial for anyone looking to achieve long-term success in their field.

Give back:

MrBeast's philanthropic efforts have been a major part of his success story, and they serve as a reminder of the importance of giving back to those in need. By using his platform to raise awareness and funds for important causes, MrBeast has shown that success and social impact can go hand in hand.

Be true to yourself:

Throughout his career, MrBeast has remained true to his unique voice and approach to content creation. He hasn't tried to be anyone other than himself, and this authenticity has been a major part of his appeal to his fans. Being true to yourself is a key ingredient for success in any field, and MrBeast's story is a testament to the power of staying true to your values and vision.

These are just a few of the key lessons that can be

gleaned from MrBeast's success story. By embracing failure, focusing on creating value, building a strong team, giving back, and staying true to yourself, anyone can achieve their own version of success, just like MrBeast has done.

HOW TO CREATE SIMILAR SUCCESS TO MRBEAST

If you're looking to create a successful YouTube channel like MrBeast, you'll need to follow a few key steps to capture your audience's attention and keep them engaged. Here are four essential tips to help you create similar success.

Step 1: Spend Your Time On Platform's Trending Section

The first step to success on YouTube is to understand what's popular on the platform. Spend time exploring the trending section to see what types of content are currently capturing people's attention. This will give you an idea of the type of content you should be creating.

For example, if you're interested in creating content about gaming, spend time exploring the gaming section of the platform. Look for videos that are getting a lot of views and engagement and try to understand why they're so popular. Then, use this information to inform your own content creation.

Another example could be exploring the food section of the platform to see what types of recipes or cooking techniques are currently popular. By understanding what's trending, you can create content that will appeal to a wide audience and increase your chances of success.

Step 2: Have A Title That Makes People Say "What The ####, Tell Me More"

The title of your video is the first thing that people will see when they come across your content. If you want to capture people's attention, you need to have a title that's catchy and intriguing. This means creating a title that makes people say "What the ####, Tell Me More".

For example, if you're creating a video about a new gaming strategy, you might use a title like "This Gaming Strategy Will Blow Your Mind". This type of title creates curiosity and makes people want to click on your video to learn more.

Another example could be creating a video about a unique food combination, such as "Mac and Cheese-Stuffed Pizza". This title is intriguing and makes people want to learn more about the unique dish.

Step 3: Have Custom Images

Custom images can make your content stand out and help it to look more professional. Use images that are related to your content and that will capture people's attention.

For example, if you're creating a video about gaming, use custom images of the game you're playing or the characters you're discussing. This will help to create a cohesive look for your content and make it more visually appealing.

Another example could be using images of the food you're cooking in your recipe videos. Custom images of the ingredients or finished dish can make your video look more professional and make people want to try the recipe for themselves.

Step 4: Make The Content Entertaining From The First Scan

People have short attention spans, so you need to capture their attention quickly if you want them to watch your entire video. Make sure your content is entertaining from the first scan.

For example, if you're creating a video about a new gaming strategy, start with a brief introduction that explains what the video will be about. Then, jump right into the strategy and start demonstrating how it works. This will keep people engaged and interested in what you're saying.

Another example could be starting your recipe video with a brief introduction of yourself and the dish you're making. Then, jump right into the cooking process and show people how to make the dish step-by-step. This will keep people engaged and interested in your video.

In conclusion, if you want to create a successful YouTube channel like MrBeast, you need to follow these four essential steps. Spend time exploring the platform's trending section to understand what's popular, create titles that make people say "What the ####, Tell Me More", use custom images to make your content look professional, and make sure your content is entertaining from the first scan. By following these steps, you can create engaging content that will capture people's attention and keep it.

THE ART OF SACRIFICE: HOW MRBEAST'S 7 YEARS HUSTLE CAN HELP YOU ACHIEVE YOUR GOALS

In today's world, everyone wants success, but very few are willing to make the necessary sacrifices. The path to success is not an easy one, and it requires a lot of hard work, dedication, and sacrifice. MrBeast, the popular YouTube star, is a prime example of what it takes to achieve success. He is known for his elaborate stunts, giveaways, and philanthropic efforts, but behind all the glitz and glamor, there is a story of dedication, perseverance, and sacrifice. In this chapter, we will explore how MrBeast's 7-year hustle can help you achieve your goals.

MrBeast continued to push the boundaries with his content, doing outrageous stunts and giving away large sums of money to his viewers.

However, behind all the success and fame, there was a lot of hard work and sacrifice. MrBeast spent countless hours creating and editing his videos, sometimes working 12-16 hours a day. He invested all his time and money into his channel, often skipping meals and living on a tight budget. He was determined to make his channel a success, no matter what it took.

The Art of Sacrifice

MrBeast's success did not come overnight; it took him seven years of hard work and sacrifice. He spent countless hours studying YouTube's algorithm, experimenting with different types of videos, and constantly learning from his mistakes. He was not afraid to take risks, even if it meant losing subscribers or receiving negative comments.

MrBeast's strategy was simple but effective: he sacrificed everything he had for his channel. He put all his energy, time, and resources into his videos, never giving up or losing faith. He understood that success was not handed to him on a silver platter, and that he had to work hard to achieve it.

The Importance of Perseverance

MrBeast's success story is a testament to the power of perseverance. He never gave up, even when things got tough. He continued to create content, even when he had few subscribers and little money. He believed in himself and his vision, and he was determined to make it a reality.

Perseverance is crucial to achieving success. It is easy to get discouraged and give up when things do not go as planned. But it is important to remember that failure is not the end; it is just a temporary setback. The key is to learn from your mistakes, make adjustments, and keep moving forward.

The Road To Success

MrBeast's story is not just a tale of sacrifice and perseverance; it is also a roadmap to success. His strategy can be broken down into three simple steps: sacrifice, perseverance, and taking risks.

Sacrifice:

To achieve success, you must be willing to sacrifice. You must be willing to invest all your time, energy, and resources into your goal. You must be willing to live on a tight budget, skip meals, and give up some of life's luxuries. Success requires sacrifice, and MrBeast's story is proof of that.

Perseverance:

Perseverance is the key to success. You must be willing to keep going, even when things get tough. Success is not achieved overnight, and setbacks and failures are a part of the journey. MrBeast's story is a perfect example of perseverance. He started his YouTube channel at the age of 13, and it took him years of hard work and dedication to gain a substantial following. He faced numerous obstacles along the way, including a lack of resources and discouragement from others. However, he persevered and continued to produce content, which ultimately paid off.

Taking Risks:

Success also requires taking risks. You must be willing to step out of your comfort zone and take calculated risks to achieve your goals. MrBeast's story is a testament to the importance of taking risks. He constantly tries new things and takes risks with his content, which has helped him stand out from other YouTubers. He also took a significant financial risk by investing a large portion of his savings into his content. While it was a risky move, it ultimately paid off, as his channel grew rapidly and became one of the most popular on YouTube.

THE FUTURE OF MRBEAST'S BRAND

MrBeast's success on YouTube and beyond has been nothing short of phenomenal, but what does the future hold for his brand? In this chapter, we'll take a closer look at where MrBeast is headed and what his plans are for the future.

One thing is clear:

MrBeast shows no signs of slowing down. He continues to push the boundaries of what is possible on YouTube and is constantly exploring new opportunities to expand his brand. Some of his recent ventures include:

MrBeast Burger:

In 2020, MrBeast launched his own virtual restaurant chain, which serves a range of burgers, fries, and other fast food items. The brand has been a massive success, with hundreds of thousands of orders in the first few months alone.

MrBeast Gaming:

In addition to his main YouTube channel, MrBeast has also launched a gaming channel, where he streams himself playing popular games like Minecraft and Among Us. The channel has already amassed millions of subscribers and is a testament to MrBeast's ability to diversify his brand.

MrBeast Philanthropy:

MrBeast's philanthropic efforts continue to be a major part of his brand. In recent years, he has donated millions of dollars to various charities and causes, and he shows no signs of slowing down. He recently announced that he would be giving away $100 million to help fight climate change, which is just the latest example of his commitment to making a positive impact on the world.

So, what's next for MrBeast? It's hard to say for sure, but it's clear that he has big plans for the future. He has hinted at the possibility of launching his own TV show, and he is always exploring new ways to engage with his audience and grow his brand. Whatever the future holds, it's clear that MrBeast will continue to be a major force in the world of online entertainment and beyond.

MrBeast's success story is an inspiring example of what is possible when you combine creativity, hard work, and a deep understanding of your audience. From his humble beginnings as a small-town teenager to his current status as one of the most successful creators on YouTube, MrBeast has proven that anything is possible if you're willing to put in the effort. And as he continues to explore new opportunities and expand his brand, there's no doubt that his influence will only continue to grow in the years to come.

The story of MrBeast is one of perseverance, innovation, and a relentless pursuit of making a positive impact on the world. From his humble beginnings creating videos in his backyard to becoming one of the most influential figures on YouTube, MrBeast has defied the odds and achieved immense success.

Through his over-the-top stunts and philanthropic efforts, MrBeast has inspired millions of fans around the world to dream big and never give up on their goals. He has shown that with hard work, determination, and a willingness to take risks and experiment, anyone can achieve their dreams and make a positive impact on the world.

Throughout this book, we have explored the various challenges that MrBeast has faced along the way, from managing his growing audience to balancing his desire for creative freedom with his philanthropic goals. We have also examined the various strategies and tactics that he has employed to overcome these challenges and continue expanding his brand and impact.

But perhaps the most important lesson that we can take away from MrBeast's story is the power of giving back. Through his various philanthropic initiatives, he has shown that success is not just about personal achievement and fame, but also about using one's platform and resources to make a positive impact on the world.

As we look to the future, it is clear that MrBeast's impact on popular culture and the broader media landscape will only continue to grow. His story is a testament to the power of hard work, determination, and a willingness to dream big and never give up on one's goals. We can all learn from his example and strive to make a positive impact on the world in our own unique way.

THE UNTOLD INSPIRATION BEHIND MRBEAST'S RECORD BREAKING SUCCESS

The world is full of stories of individuals who have risen from humble beginnings to achieve great things. Among these tales of triumph, few are as compelling as that of MrBeast, the YouTube sensation who has captured the hearts of millions with his unique brand of content and philanthropy.

So, what inspired MrBeast to become the force for good that he is today? What led him to use his success to help others, rather than simply accumulating wealth and fame for himself? To answer these questions, we must look at the influences and experiences that have shaped his life.

One of the most significant inspirations in MrBeast's life has been his grandfather, who he credits with teaching him the importance of hard work and generosity.

Growing up, MrBeast would often help his grandfather with odd jobs around his farm, learning the value of putting in a hard day's work and treating others with kindness and respect.

Another important influence in MrBeast's life has been his faith. As a devout Christian, he has spoken openly about the role that his beliefs have played in shaping his worldview and motivating him to give back to others. In a world that can often seem cold and uncaring, MrBeast's faith has given him a sense of purpose and direction, and has driven him to use his platform to make a positive impact on the world.

In addition to these personal inspirations, MrBeast has also been motivated by a desire to prove the naysayers wrong. As he has grown his platform and achieved unprecedented success, he has faced criticism from some who have accused him of being frivolous or irresponsible with his spending. However, rather than being discouraged by these criticisms, MrBeast has used them as fuel to redouble his efforts and prove that he can use his platform for good.

THE INFLUENTIAL YOUTUBERS WHO HAVE SHAPED MRBEAST'S RISE TO SUCCESS

As MrBeast's meteoric rise to fame continues, many have begun to wonder about the sources of his inspiration. While it's clear that he has an innovative and creative mind all his own, it's also true that he draws upon a range of influences in crafting his videos and building his brand. In this chapter, we'll explore some of the key figures in the YouTube space who have inspired MrBeast's work, and examine what lessons he has learned from them.

First on our list of inspirations is none other than PewDiePie, the reigning king of YouTube with over 110 million subscribers. MrBeast has spoken in interviews about the influence that PewDiePie's style of humor and storytelling has had on his own content, and it's not hard to see the similarities between the two creators. Both are masters of absurd humor, often employing shock value and unexpected twists to keep their audiences engaged. But beyond that, PewDiePie has also been an inspiration to MrBeast in his approach to community building. The Swede is known for his close relationship with his fans, and MrBeast has similarly made an effort to engage with his followers and build a sense of community around his channel.

Another key influence on MrBeast has been the YouTube gaming community as a whole. While he doesn't focus exclusively on gaming content, his early videos were often centered around popular games like Minecraft and Fortnite. In this regard, MrBeast has taken inspiration from a number of prominent gamers and gaming channels, such as Markiplier, Jacksepticeye, and Ninja. These creators have helped to define the language and culture of gaming on YouTube, and MrBeast has drawn on their example in crafting his own videos. He has also been inspired by the gaming community's ethos of hard work and dedication, and has often cited his own relentless work ethic as a key factor in his success.

Beyond the gaming world, MrBeast has also taken inspiration from a variety of other YouTube channels and personalities. For example, he has cited the tech-focused channel Linus Tech Tips as an inspiration in terms of production values and attention to detail. Meanwhile, he has drawn on the work of educational channels like Vsauce and Kurzgesagt in crafting videos that are both informative and engaging. And of course, he has also been inspired by fellow creators within his own niche of "stunt" videos, such as The Slow Mo Guys and Dude Perfect.

But perhaps the most important source of inspiration for MrBeast has been his own life experiences. From a young age, he has been drawn to entrepreneurship and the idea of making something out of nothing. As he has grown his brand on YouTube, he has drawn on this experience and drive to continually innovate and push the boundaries of what's possible on the platform. He has also been shaped by his experiences as a member of Gen Z, growing up in a world where social media and online content are ubiquitous. In this sense, MrBeast's work can be seen as a reflection of the unique cultural moment in which we find ourselves, as well as a product of his own innate talents and drive.

So what lessons can we learn from MrBeast's inspirations? Perhaps the most important is the value of hard work and dedication. Whether drawing on the gaming community's work ethic or the example of other successful creators, MrBeast has always emphasized the importance of putting in the time and effort to achieve one's goals. Another key lesson is the value of community building and engagement. By following in the footsteps of PewDiePie and other prominent creators, MrBeast has built a loyal following of fans who feel invested in his success.

This success is a product of his unique blend of talent, hard work, and inspiration from other successful YouTubers. By studying the techniques of those who came before him and adapting them to his own style, he has built an empire that continues to grow and evolve.

As Robert Greene writes in "Mastery", "The future belongs to those who learn more skills and combine them in creative ways." MrBeast's ability to learn from the best and create his own unique style is a testament to this idea. He has shown that by studying the successes of others and adapting their methods to fit his own goals, anyone can achieve great things.

In the end, MrBeast's journey is a reminder that success is not a destination, but a continuous journey of growth and self-improvement. By embracing the lessons of those who came before us and constantly striving to learn and innovate, we can all achieve our own version of success, just like MrBeast.

BONUS: MRBEAST'S ASTROLOGY AND NUMEROLOGY PROFILING DECODED

A strology and numerology have been used for centuries to gain insights into a person's personality, strengths, and weaknesses. Astrology focuses on the positions of celestial bodies at the time of birth, while numerology analyzes the numerical values assigned to letters in a person's name and birthdate. By decoding these profiles, we can gain a deeper understanding of individuals and their potential for success.

MrBeast, one of the most successful YouTubers of our time, has captivated millions with his incredible videos and philanthropic endeavors. By examining his birth chart, we can gain insights into his personality traits and motivations. MrBeast was born on May 7, 1998, making him a Taurus with a strong sense of determination and practicality. Taurus individuals are known for their hard work and ability to manifest their goals into reality.

In addition to astrology, numerology plays a significant role in MrBeast's profile. By analyzing the numerical values assigned to letters in his name and birthdate, we can uncover his life path number, which provides insights into his purpose and potential. MrBeast's life path number is 1, indicating strong leadership qualities and a drive for success. This number suggests that he is destined to make a significant impact on the world.

Astrology and numerology not only shed light on MrBeast's personality but also influence his content creation. As a Taurus, he is drawn to practical and tangible experiences, which is evident in his videos that often involve real-life challenges and acts of kindness. His life path number of 1 gives him the confidence and determination to take risks and push boundaries, allowing him to create unique and attention-grabbing content.

MrBeast's success can be attributed, in part, to the alignment of his astrological traits and numerological profile. His Taurus nature provides him with a strong work ethic and practical mindset, while his life path number 1 fuels his ambition and desire to make a difference. By understanding the astrological and numerological factors behind his success, we can gain valuable insights into the strategies that have propelled him to the top.

While astrology and numerology may not guarantee success, they can serve as valuable tools for self-reflection and understanding. By analyzing your own birth chart and numerology profile, you can gain insights into your strengths, weaknesses, and potential areas for growth. This understanding can help you tailor your content strategy to align with your unique traits and aspirations, increasing your chances of creating meaningful and impactful content.

There are numerous online tools and resources available for astrology and numerology profiling. Websites such as AstroSeek and Cafe Astrology provide free birth chart calculators and detailed interpretations of astrological placements. For numerology, websites like Numerology.com offer free calculations and insights into life path numbers, destiny numbers, and more. These resources can serve as a starting point for your own self-discovery journey.

MrBeast is not the only successful YouTuber whose astrology and numerology profiles contribute to their achievements. By examining case studies of other content creators, we can see how astrology and numerology have influenced their paths to success. From the fiery nature of Aries to the innovative mindset of Aquarius, each individual's astrological and numerological traits play a role in shaping their content and attracting their audience.

While astrology and numerology provide insightful guidance, it is important to remember that they are just tools. Success in content creation ultimately stems from a combination of passion, hard work, and strategic planning. However, by understanding your astrological and numerological profiles, you can gain a deeper understanding of yourself and utilize this knowledge to create content that resonates with your audience on a profound level.

Astrology and numerology offer valuable insights into MrBeast's personality traits and motivations, shedding light on the strategies that have contributed to his immense success. By applying these principles to your own content strategy and utilizing the available tools and resources, you can gain a deeper understanding of yourself and create content that aligns with your unique strengths. While astrology and numerology are not guarantees for success, they can serve as valuable tools for self-reflection and personal growth in the ever-evolving world of content creation.

CONCLUSION

As we conclude this book on the success story of MrBeast, it's worth taking a moment to reflect on some of the key lessons we can learn from his experiences.Firstly, it's important to understand that money is not everything, but it certainly can make a significant difference in our lives. However, the way we approach money and the mindset we have towards it can determine whether it brings us happiness or misery. MrBeast's approach to money is refreshing because he understands the value of using it to help others and make a positive impact on the world. He is a firm believer in the concept of giving, and he is always looking for ways to use his wealth to make a difference in the lives of those around him.Furthermore, MrBeast's success is a testament to the fact that those who know how to manage their money and give to the right people will attract even more money. It's not just about accumulating wealth for oneself, but about using it wisely and strategically to create even more opportunities for success and growth.In addition to his generosity, MrBeast's success also comes from his investment in creating content that people enjoy and want to watch. He has a unique talent for capturing people's attention and keeping them engaged, and he uses this talent to create entertaining and informative content that has attracted millions of viewers and subscribers. As we all know, we will all die one day, and the legacy we leave behind is what truly matters. MrBeast understands this concept well, and he is focused on creating a positive impact on the world that will outlive him. He is using his platform and his resources to make a difference, and this is something we can all learn from.The success story of MrBeast teaches us the importance of having a positive mindset towards money and using it wisely to create opportunities for growth and impact. Giving is an essential aspect of this, and we should always strive to use our resources to help others and make a positive impact on the world. By doing so, we can create a lasting legacy that will inspire others for generations to come.

EPILOGUE

The story of MrBeast is a testament to the power of hard work, dedication, and strategic thinking. His success is not just about making money, but also about using that money to make a positive impact on the world.

By giving away millions of dollars to charity, MrBeast has shown that money can be a force for good when used wisely. He has also demonstrated the importance of investing in oneself, surrounding oneself with the right people, and constantly pushing oneself out of one's comfort zone.

Ultimately, the key takeaway from MrBeast's story is that success is not just about achieving one's own goals, but also about using that success to help others. By giving back to society and investing in the future, we can all make a difference in the world.

So, let us all strive to follow in MrBeast's footsteps by working hard, managing our money wisely, and giving back to those in need. By doing so, we can achieve our own goals while also making a positive impact on the world around us.

AFTERWORD

As I reflect back on the journey of MrBeast and the lessons learned from his success, I cannot help but be reminded of the importance of hard work, persistence, and a willingness to take risks. MrBeast's story shows us that with these qualities, anyone can achieve their dreams and create a life that is both fulfilling and rewarding.

One of the most important takeaways from MrBeast's success is the importance of having a clear vision and purpose. MrBeast was able to build a successful brand and career because he knew exactly what he wanted to achieve and was willing to put in the work necessary to make it happen. His ability to stay focused on his goals, despite the challenges and obstacles he faced, is a testament to the power of having a clear vision for your life.

Another key lesson from MrBeast's journey is the importance of giving back and investing in others. MrBeast has shown us that when we give to others, we not only make a positive impact on their lives but also on our own. By investing in others and helping them achieve their own dreams and goals, we create a ripple effect of positivity and success that can benefit everyone involved.

Finally, MrBeast's story teaches us the value of managing our finances wisely and using our resources to make a positive impact on the world. Money is not everything, but it can be a powerful tool for creating change and making a difference in the world. By investing in causes that are important to us and using our resources to help others, we can create a legacy that will last long after we are gone.

ACKNOWLEDGEMENT

Writing this book about MrBeast has been a truly enlightening and inspiring experience. I am grateful for the opportunity to delve into the life and career of such a remarkable individual, and to share his story with others.

I would like to express my heartfelt thanks to MrBeast himself, for his generosity in sharing his time and insights. with me. Without him, this book would not have been possible.

I would also like to thank my editor, who provided invaluable guidance and support throughout the writing process, as well as my friends and family, who have encouraged me every step of the way.

Finally, I would like to thank the readers of this book, for their interest and curiosity about MrBeast and the world of YouTube. It is my hope that this book has provided both entertainment and inspiration, and that it will encourage others to pursue their passions with the same dedication and drive as MrBeast himself.

Made in the USA
Columbia, SC
01 March 2024

32515123R00078